Kenilworth Castle

Richard K Morris

Introduction

Kenilworth Castle is one of the great historical sites of the United Kingdom. It was a royal castle for most of its history, and many of the buildings remain unaltered since the reign of Queen Elizabeth I. Its walls enclose a series of outstanding works of medieval and early Renaissance architecture.

Set on a low sandstone hill, protected by marshes at the confluence of the Finham and Inchford brooks, the first castle was established in the 1120s by the royal chamberlain, Geoffrey de Clinton. He built most of the Norman keep and also founded Kenilworth Priory close by. In the early 13th century King John added an outer circuit of stone walls and a dam to hold back a great lake, thus creating one of the most formidable fortresses in the kingdom. It withstood a full-scale siege in 1266.

Subsequently the castle was developed as a palace. John of Gaunt, son of King Edward III, constructed the great hall, with associated apartments and services. In the 15th century, the castle was a favoured residence of the Lancastrian kings, who were drawn here by the excellent hunting. King Henry V built a retreat called 'the Pleasance in the Marsh' at the far end of the lake. In 1563, Elizabeth I granted the castle to her favourite, Robert Dudley, earl of Leicester. He converted Kenilworth into a great prodigy house for her entertainment, which culminated in 19 days of festivities in 1575.

The castle's fortifications were dismantled in 1650 after the Civil War. Leicester's Gatehouse was converted into a residence by the Parliamentarian officer, Colonel Hawkesworth. In 1821, the ivy-clad ruins became famous as the setting for Sir Walter Scott's novel, *Kenilworth*, which romanticised the story of Robert Dudley, Queen Elizabeth and Amy Robsart. The castle was given by Lord Kenilworth to the town of Kenilworth in 1958, and since 1984 it has been managed by English Heritage.

Above: *Robert Dudley, earl of Leicester, from a miniature by Nicholas Hilliard, 1571–4*

Facing page: *Kenilworth Castle from the south-west, in late afternoon sunshine, which brings out the warm tones of the sandstone. John of Gaunt's buildings are to the left and centre, with the keep behind, and Leicester's Building to the right. For the same view painted by Turner in about 1830, see page 33*

The Tour

Kenilworth Castle is one of the most impressive castles in the country and has played host to King Edward I, King Henry V, Queen Elizabeth I and Queen Victoria. Its spectacular ruins reveal much of its medieval and Tudor past. The tour covers the extensive outer defences, the keep, the remains of the magnificent residential accommodation, the gatehouse, the stable and the Tudor garden.

FOLLOWING THE TOUR

The tour of the castle starts just outside the ticket office and shop. The numbers beside the headings highlight the key points on the tour and correspond with the small numbered plans in the margins.

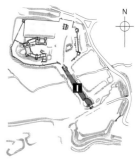

❚ EXTERIOR AND OUTLYING FEATURES

The view from just outside the visitor centre provides a splendid visual introduction to the castle. The main buildings stand on a low sandstone hill above the confluence of the Finham and Inchford brooks. When the Norman castle was built, the construction of a causeway across this valley created a dam which held back a lake (known as the mere) to the west. This was vastly enlarged when King John heightened the dam in the early 13th century. A little further down the valley was the abbey pool adjoining Kenilworth Priory, the monastery founded about 1124 at the same time as the castle (see page 36). The top of the dam was later widened to make it suitable for jousting at tournaments, and by the mid-16th century it was referred to as the 'tiltyard'.

Standing on the tiltyard today, the visitor needs to imagine the great mere stretching into the middle distance to the left. Behind (towards the car-park) lie the remains of the defences and water controls essential to the security and maintenance of the mere. Close to the ticket office and shop are the fragmentary remains of the Gallery Tower and its courtyard, part of the gatehouse which guarded the southern end of the dam. It takes its name from a remodelling in the 16th century as a viewing gallery for tournaments. Beyond lies the large defensive outwork of the Brays, in which the car-park is situated, with the line of its banks and ditches now marked by the arc of tall trees. The name may refer to the 'bays' or ponds of water in the vicinity, but a more likely derivation is from the French 'braie', meaning a military outwork defended by palisades.

Above: The castle buildings seen from the tiltyard

Below: A scene from the great tournament held at Westminster by King Henry VIII on New Year's Day, 1511. For jousting, the tiltyard at Kenilworth would have had a barrier like this down the centre, and spectators looked on from the towers at each end

Facing page: The southern towers of the inner court, seen from the outer court: the Saintlowe Tower (left), Gaunt's Tower (centre) and the south-west turret of Leicester's Building (right)

Right: The castle buildings seen over the outer curtain wall, with the ruins of Leicester's Building in the centre
Below: The remains of the twin towers of Mortimer's Tower, the main gatehouse to the medieval castle, as seen from the tiltyard

Facing page: Kenilworth Castle as it appeared in 1620, in an 18th-century copy of a lost 17th-century wall-painting at Newnham Paddox House, Warwickshire. This naïve painting shows the castle with its mere and pools before the dismantling of 1650, with the tiltyard (left), the inner court with the lost King Henry's Lodgings (centre) and the garden site (right)

❷ MORTIMER'S TOWER

Proceeding to the far end of the tiltyard, the visitor arrives at Mortimer's Tower.

This was the main medieval entrance to the castle. The name derives from Sir William Dugdale, the 17th-century antiquary, and probably

relates to Roger Mortimer, who hosted a tournament at the castle in 1279. It is still possible to make out the two D-shaped towers of the gatehouse, built as part of King John's ring of stone defences for the outer bailey between about 1210 and 1215. Originally the towers were at least one storey higher. They would have had battlements, and were linked by an entrance passage.

In the passage, grooves survive for a medieval portcullis, which would have been operated by a winch in the room above. A door on each side led to 'two porter's lodges' fitted with fireplaces, according to the survey of the castle made in 1563. King John's gatehouse was built in front of a simpler, 12th-century gatehouse. The walls of this earlier building are preserved at the inner end of the passage, along with another portcullis slot. Even in their mutilated form, both gatehouses are significant survivals of fortifications from their respective periods.

Like so much else of the castle, Mortimer's Tower was dismantled in 1650, following the Civil War.

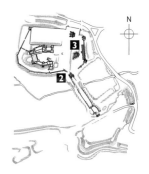

❸ OUTER COURT

The visitor should now proceed through Mortimer's Tower to the 'base court', the lowest part of the outer court. On the right is the 16th-century stable, which houses an introductory exhibition about the castle. In front of the stable are the foundations of the 14th-century chapel of St Mary. The ruined Water Tower is to the right of the stable and beyond the stable are the ruins of Lunn's Tower (see page 31). Through the trees in the distance is Leicester's Gatehouse (see page 28). The avenue of trees was planted only about 150 years ago, to enhance the picturesque setting of the ruins.

On the higher ground rises the monumental group of buildings of the inner court. The great tower to the right is the keep built by Geoffrey de Clinton in the 1120s, which was at the heart of the defences of the Norman castle, and also served as its main residence. In the centre beyond is the 14th-century great hall, built by John of Gaunt between about 1373 and 1380. The towering block to the left is Leicester's Building, erected to provide private apartments for Elizabeth I in 1571. It was consciously designed as a foil to the ancient keep. Together they present a façade to the outer court which is harmonious in overall form yet varied in detail; the massive solidity of the keep contrasts with the delicate windows of Leicester's Building – a typically Elizabethan conceit.

In the 16th century, these two towers were linked by a lower east range, named by Dugdale 'King Henry's Lodgings', which would have hidden the inner court from view. The lodgings, built between about 1530 and 1532, was a two-storey, timber-framed building erected in Henry VIII's reign, on the line of the inner bailey wall and probably replacing a previous range which had decayed. Its likely purpose was to improve the private apartments and to provide additional lodgings. It is documented that window glass was brought from London in 1531–2, painted with the badges and arms of the king, and it might have been intended for this building. King Henry's Lodgings is depicted with a series of bay windows in the painting below. It was demolished at the slighting of the castle in 1650.

▣ INNER COURT

In Tudor times, visitors would have entered the inner court at its north-east corner, through a gatehouse between the keep and King Henry's Lodgings. In front of the entrance are the foundations of one side of a causeway and the springing for a bridge across the former dry ditch. On the arrival of Elizabeth I on 9 July 1575, this bridge was decorated with symbolic gifts for her from the Roman gods and goddesses, such as Mars (war), Bacchus (wine) and Phoebus (music), arranged on seven pairs of posts.

The visitor should now proceed uphill, past the site of the former gate. Though the architecture of the inner court ranges in date from the 1120s to the 1570s, a sense of harmony pervades the ensemble. This may, in part, be due to the use of the same mellow red sandstone, from quarries adjacent to the castle. However, conscious architectural devices have also been employed, such as the way the tall sloping plinth of the 14th-century hall makes reference to the great stepped plinth of the keep.

THE SOUTH-EAST TURRET OF THE KEEP

1 Remains of the entrance gate to the inner court

2 Portcullis groove

3 Scar for the battlemented parapet of the wall-walk

4 16th-century door giving access to the top of King Henry's Lodgings

Below: A reconstruction of the castle as it might have appeared about 1575, viewed from the east

Facing page: Leicester's Building (left) and the keep, seen from the outer court

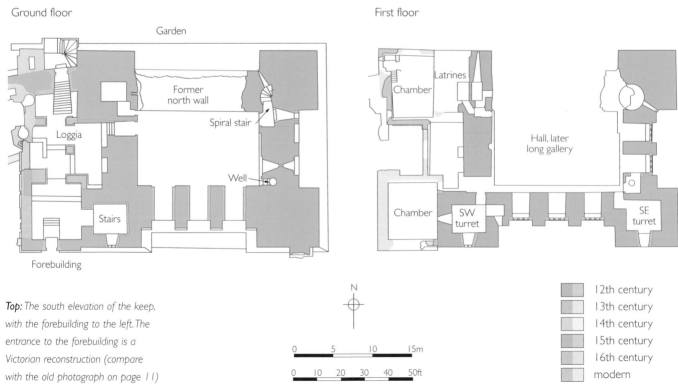

Ground floor

Garden

Former
north wall

Spiral stair

Loggia

Well

Stairs

Forebuilding

First floor

Chamber

Latrines

Hall, later
long gallery

Chamber

SW
turret

SE
turret

N

0   5   10   15m

0 10 20 30 40 50ft

12th century
13th century
14th century
15th century
16th century
modern

Top: *The south elevation of the keep, with the forebuilding to the left. The entrance to the forebuilding is a Victorian reconstruction (compare with the old photograph on page 11)*

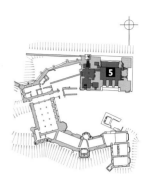

5 KEEP AND FOREBUILDING

Facing the keep from the centre of the inner court, it is not difficult to appreciate why this massive building was always at the heart of the castle's defence. It was also successively used for residence, administration and entertainment.

Exterior

On the side facing the inner court (the south), three main periods of building are evident. First, the two main floors of the structure were probably built by Geoffrey de Clinton in the 1120s. In the centre section his work extends up to the foot of the arrowloops. Second, most of the top stage was added by King John between about 1210 and 1215 and is characterised by the fish-tailed arrowloops, which were an innovative development to accommodate the use of the crossbow. King John was also responsible for a chamber with fine views at the top of the south-west turret. Third, the three Elizabethan grid windows were introduced by Robert Dudley, earl of Leicester, about 1570 or 1571, to light a great room for entertaining on the first floor. At the

top of the south-east (right) turret are the peg-holes for the square face of the castle clock, which was stopped at two o'clock throughout Queen Elizabeth's visit in 1575.

Adjoining the keep on the left is the forebuilding, which provided additional security and a grand ceremonial entry. High above the entry to the forebuilding, abutting the keep, is the jamb of a tall oriel window, which once lit a fine first-floor chamber. The jamb is decorated with Leicester's badges, the cinquefoil and the ragged staff, and below it, the date '[1]570'. Unusually, these carvings have been done after construction, so the window probably pre-dates 1570, and might have been built by Leicester in about 1568, or by his father, John Dudley, earl of Northumberland, between 1549 and 1553.

Interior

Now enter the forebuilding through the restored, round-arched doorway. The classical arcades of the loggia dominate the interior of the forebuilding. They were inserted in the 16th century to create a fashionable approach to the

Below, left: The date '[1]570' carved on the forebuilding
Below, bottom left: The keep at Castle Rising (Norfolk), built about 1140, preserves a good example of a Norman forebuilding
Below, right: This photograph of about 1860 shows the decayed state of the forebuilding and the south-west turret of the keep before later 19th-century restoration

garden beyond. Originally, the forebuilding would have been an enclosed space, with a staircase going up to the first-floor entrance into the keep. However, later changes make it impossible now to reconstruct the Norman arrangement in detail. Roof-lines on the north face of the corner turret, and large beam-holes in the wall of the keep, testify to various remodellings of the forebuilding. In the 13th century, it was extended north to provide a sally-port to the outer bailey, later serving as the door to the garden.

Go up the wooden stairs to enter the keep through a round-headed door in the west wall. This door may always have been accessible from the forebuilding, suggesting that defence was not the sole purpose of this structure. Inside the keep, one can see that this monumental building consisted of two lofty floors with a fighting deck above. Its walls are 14 feet (4.3m) thick, as shown by the scars of the north wall demolished in 1650. During the 12th century, the keep was probably the main residence of the castle, centred on a great hall occupying the upper floor. The hall was an undivided space entered from the forebuilding by the large door in the west wall on the first floor, with a massive roof spanning about 30 feet (9m). The hall was well appointed, with a well in its south-east corner and spiral stairs in the north-east turret, giving access to all levels. Latrines in the north-west turret were accessed through the round-arched door in the west wall, close to which is a small, restored 12th-century fireplace.

The hall was lit by large, round-arched windows, probably like the restored examples in the west wall. They are likely to be modifications made in the 1170s or 1180s by King Henry II and, if reliably restored, are remarkable in size for a 12th-century keep. Leading off the hall were chambers in the south-east and south-west turrets; the former might have housed a chapel. A payment was made in 1444–5 for adapting the chapel to store 'evidences' (documents), indicating an administrative function for the keep in the 15th century. Between 1570 and 1571 Leicester remodelled the upper floor, possibly to serve as the equivalent of an Elizabethan long gallery, where some of his notable collection of paintings might have been displayed (see feature on page 26).

The lower floor of the keep (where the visitor stands) was separated from the upper hall by a wooden ceiling supported on intermediate supports. This floor originally supplied additional accommodation for the household. The Norman slit window in the east wall shows how dark it would have been until Leicester opened up the window apertures in the south wall.

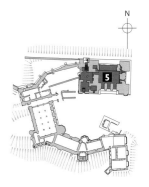

THE INTERIOR OF THE KEEP, LOOKING EAST

1 Door to the stairs
2 Original Norman window
3 Ground-floor access to the well
4 Spiral staircase
5 First-floor doors to the well and south-east turret
6 Elizabethan windows inserted into 12th-century apertures

Facing page: The loggia leading to the garden, seen from the entrance to the forebuilding. The arcades supported three lofty chambers above, arranged round a small courtyard

Above: The keep and the site of the kitchens, seen from the Strong Tower
Below: The back of a kitchen fireplace, repaired with reused medieval church floor tiles
Below right: The east fireplace of the kitchen, with bread oven and copper

6 JOHN OF GAUNT'S WORKS

Retrace your route through the forebuilding and back to the inner court, to face John of Gaunt's great hall. This hall, and the buildings to the left and right, called 'Lancaster's Buildings' by Dugdale, were erected between about 1373 and 1380. They represent the finest survival of an English royal palace of the later Middle Ages and one of the clearest expressions of the organisation of a great aristocratic household in the period. The household was run by the chamberlain, the steward, the treasurer and the clerk of the wardrobe. Gaunt's household numbered over 100 male servants, many of aristocratic birth, whose primary purpose was to maintain the magnificence of his public image.

7 KITCHENS

Proceed into the area of the former kitchens and services. The structures of the kitchens have almost entirely disappeared; they would probably have been largely of timber-framed construction. Presumably, there had been a kitchen here since at least the 13th century, but the existing kitchens appear to be substantially the work of John of Gaunt.

The main kitchen was a long rectangular hall, 66 feet (19m) by 28 feet (8.5m), built against the earlier curtain wall. Remarkably, it was twice the size of a normal aristocratic kitchen. The hearths of its three enormous fireplaces are preserved, with smaller recesses in between for storing wood and utensils. The foundation of the other side-wall

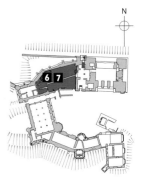

is visible, together with a cobbled floor with a drain in the centre for kitchen waste. In the east wall is a fourth fireplace, equipped with a bread oven on the left, and a furnace on the right for a built-in copper, or cauldron, for boiling chunks of meat. The copper is a modification, probably introduced in the later 15th century. This kitchen had the capacity to cater for several hundred people if necessary, but the east fireplace alone would have been adequate for the skeleton staff when the lord was not in residence.

The southern part of the kitchen area was occupied by the privy kitchen, where food was prepared for the lord, his family and special guests. It was hidden from the inner court by a tall wall against the hall stairs, and the only trace of it today is the hearth in this wall.

The services also included a pantry, buttery, larder, pastry and scullery. The pastry, where hard pastry cases were baked to serve as containers for food, was probably to the left of the door into the Strong Tower cellars, and is a later addition. Between the kitchens and the stone steps was a dresser, where the food from the kitchen was

Left: Reconstruction of the copper, with steps to enable a cook to reach into it
Below: The late medieval kitchen at Windsor Castle, as depicted by James Stephanoff in the 19th century, gives a good impression of a top-lit kitchen with massive fireplaces like Kenilworth's

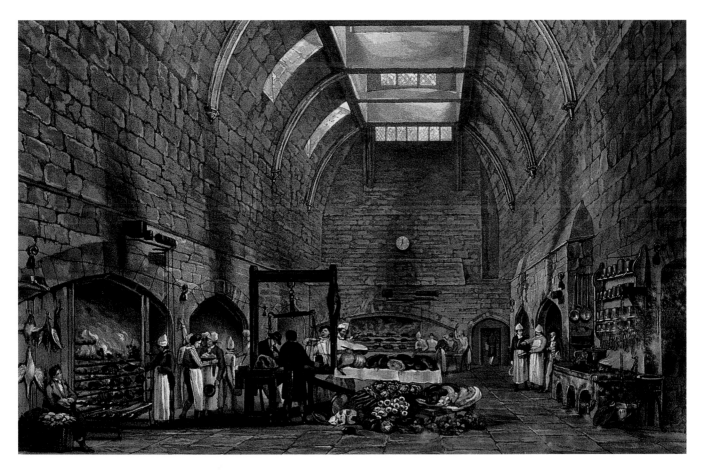

arranged, before being carried up the stairs (on the line of the present wooden staircase) and through a passage into the hall.

8 STRONG TOWER

The name 'a strong tower' appears in a survey of the castle made in 1545, presumably alluding to the remarkable feature that all its floors were vaulted in stone. The stone-vaulted cellars of the tower, which feel like dungeons, actually housed the larders.

The visitor should now climb the wooden staircase to the first floor of the Strong Tower. This was occupied by the buttery and the pantry, separated by the passage from the kitchen. The buttery contained the supplies of ale and wine, decanted for use in the hall, and the pantry contained the bread supplies. The buttery, the kitchen passage and the pantry emerged into the screens passage of the hall through three separate doors; the stone jamb of the right-hand door survives.

A further wooden staircase takes the visitor to the second floor, passing over the base of a spiral staircase, which was the original means of access upstairs. The surviving room was the inner chamber of a suite of lodgings, equipped with a fireplace. The polygonal room in the turret served as a bedchamber, and later provided the inspiration to Sir Walter Scott for Amy Robsart's 'small octangular chamber' in 'Mervyn's Tower', during her fictional stay at Kenilworth. The lodgings were designed for a senior household officer, probably the steward, because the various spiral stairs gave him direct access to the services and to the hall.

The visitor should now leave the lodgings by the south door leading to the south-west spiral staircase. From the stairs, visitors can go down to two strong-rooms, which were probably used for storing pewter, plate and other valuable items needed in the hall. Visitors should also go up to the top of the tower, where the best panoramic views of the castle and the site of the mere are to be found. The Pleasance lay at the far end of the mere, beyond where the group of buildings at High House Farm now stands in the middle distance. Originally the tower was one storey higher, like the Saintlowe Tower to the left.

Now retrace your route to ground level, and walk through the kitchens to stand in front of the great hall.

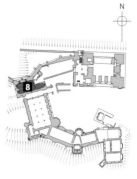

Left: The cellars of the Strong Tower
Facing page: The great hall, seen from the west, with the Strong Tower (left) and Saintlowe Tower (right)

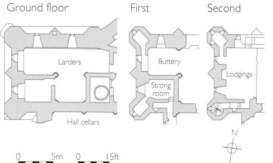

Ground floor — Larders, Hall cellars
First — Buttery, Strong room
Second — Lodgings

0 5m 0 15ft

THE STRONG TOWER AND SERVICES

1 Site of the dresser and stairs to the hall

2 Entrance to the cellars

3 Site of the buttery and pantry

4 Steward's lodgings and 'Amy Robsart's chamber'

THE EAST SIDE OF THE HALL

1 Hall cellars

2 Entrance to the hall

3 Perpendicular window tracery

4 Fireplace with wall above for tapestry

5 Large wall-slots for the roof trusses

6 Site of the bay window

9 GREAT HALL

John of Gaunt's great hall was the architectural masterpiece of the inner court, designed to symbolise his regal status. It is no wonder that this was the only part of the castle left unaltered by Leicester 200 years later, for it entirely suited the image he wished to project.

Exterior

The building is six bays long, with the bay window on the left balanced by the porch on the right. The windows are noteworthy both for their exceptional height and for their delicacy; they are more like cathedral windows. Each one is divided by horizontal transoms into three sections. The rectangular lights were originally barred and shuttered, while the tracery in the upper section had the luxury of fixed glazing. This tracery is the best surviving example of the early Perpendicular style in a domestic building. It is similar to the tracery in the contemporary chapter house of the earl of Warwick's new collegiate foundation at St Mary's, Warwick.

The hall itself was on the first floor, raised over stone-vaulted cellars, and its porch was

originally approached up a long straight stair of 20 steps. The entrance arch, which is ostentatiously carved with rows of foliage, led into the screens passage at the low end of the hall.

Right: The entrance doorway of the hall porch, with carved foliage decoration in its arch

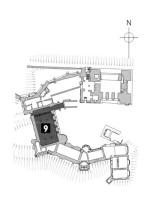

Interior

Visitors should now proceed through the ground-floor entrance to stand on the site of the cellars. Here, there were two rows of pillars at 15 feet (4.6m) intervals, supporting the rib-vaulting on which the hall floor once rested. The north end of the cellars was taken up by a cross-passage to a small exit, secured by a portcullis, which provided an alternative route from the inner court to a gate on the edge of the mere. In the 1563 survey, the wine cellar and the beer cellar occupied the rest of the space under the hall, like the contemporary arrangement at Hampton Court Palace.

Above, the magnificent interior of the hall was dominated by its deep-set windows, all of which featured panelled surrounds and stone seats. Benches would have been put against the walls to create a step up to the seats, from which spectators could watch entertainments after a banquet. The bare panels of wall above the fireplaces would have been hung with tapestries, which were among the most prized possessions of 14th-century aristocrats. Gaunt's hall was exceptional in once having no fewer than six fireplaces. Besides the two surviving fireplaces, there was a row of three more fireplaces on the far wall. This feature was at the cutting edge of architectural fashion. The hall of Gaunt's eldest brother, the Black Prince, at Kennington Palace in Surrey, dating from about 1358, probably had a

Left: Reconstruction of the interior of the great hall, looking from the screens passage end. The first-floor entrance to the hall is at the left, and the vaulted cellars in the cutaway at the right. Circular fire-screens are set in the fireplace openings behind the high table, with a canopy of honour and a tapestry above. The reconstruction of the timber roof is speculative

Gaunt retained his own company of musicians. His hall probably had a minstrels' gallery over the screens passage, and one definitely existed in Leicester's time.

The rapid pace of change in 14th-century architectural fashion is shown by the fact that Gaunt's hall was the third on this site in 60 years. Thomas, earl of Lancaster, built a 'new hall' in 1313–14, which would have been a ground-floor hall, with internal arcades to support the roof. In 1347 Henry of Lancaster had the hall remodelled. A London carpenter, Richard de Felstede, was contracted to make a new roof, which suggests a major work, probably involving the removal of the arcades and the creation of a single-span roof.

A generation later, Gaunt had Henry's hall almost totally rebuilt (between 1373 and 1380) so as to raise it on cellars, on the model of Edward III's new hall at Windsor. Some features from the 1347 hall might have been reused, such as the carved stone entrance doorway, but the roof was apparently replaced. No record of its design survives, but it remained the widest roof of any royal hall in medieval and Tudor England, save only for the quite exceptional roof of Westminster great hall. Like Westminster, externally it would have been

similar triple fireplace. The sixth fireplace at Kenilworth is in the bay window.

The duke would have dined in the hall only on the most important of occasions. The food would have been brought in through a wooden screen at the kitchen end. The serving of food was the most elaborate ritual which took place in the hall, permitting a lavish display of hospitality. Musical accompaniment was a significant feature, and

Above: A magnificent example of a triple fireplace in the hall of John of Gaunt's contemporary, the duke of Berry, in his palace at Poitiers, France (1380s)
Right: The medieval roof of St George's Hall, Windsor, gives an impression of how the Kenilworth hall might have looked (engraving of a Garter Feast by Wenceslaus Hollar, about 1668)

high-pitched in the tradition of great halls – a visible external symbol of wealth and hospitality.

10 SAINTLOWE TOWER

Visitors should now walk across the hall site to enter the ground floor of the Saintlowe Tower. The name was used by Sir Walter Scott for a fictitious Norman founder of the castle. The ground floor was a wine cellar, used to supply wine to the high end of the hall, by way of the corner stairs. Visitors should now go up the stairs.

The first floor forms a gallery with large windows and fitted seats looking over the chase and the mere. The stairs originally continued to a superior set of lodgings on the second floor. These might have been for the chamberlain, who was in charge of the apartments and private chambers. In the space below was a lodging for another official, perhaps the clerk of the wardrobe.

A good view of the range of state apartments is gained from the first floor of the Saintlowe Tower. The further away the apartments were from the hall, the greater their exclusiveness. This gallery once led to the first apartment, the great chamber. At the far end of the great chamber was a lobby, linking to the second chamber.

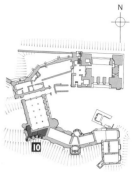

Left: The Saintlowe Tower seen from the outer court. The large windows are for the viewing gallery
Below: The hall bay window (left) and the site of the state apartments, seen from the first floor of the Saintlowe Tower

Right: The range of apartments, seen from the top of the keep. The site of the great chamber is in the centre, flanked by Gaunt's Tower (left) and the hall bay window and the Saintlowe Tower (right)

▥ STATE APARTMENTS

Visitors should now retrace their route to the inner court and proceed across it to stand near the front of the oriel, the central feature of the apartment range.

GAUNT'S TOWER

Third floor

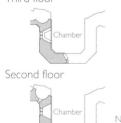
Chamber

Second floor

Chamber

First floor

Hall place

N

Ground floor
Lobby

Latrine

0   5m   0   15ft

Exterior

The state apartments were on the first floor, and are difficult to appreciate now because their fabric has been almost totally removed after 1650. They can be reconstructed from surveys of the castle taken in 1545 and 1563, though room names and functions changed somewhat between the 14th and 17th centuries. The three main rooms were the great chamber, the second chamber (1545) or presence chamber (1563), and the privy chamber.

The features still standing provide evidence for two main periods of work: Gaunt's and Leicester's. The oriel, Gaunt's Tower behind it, the great chamber and probably the second chamber were all built for John of Gaunt in the 1370s. The great chamber is on the site of an earlier chamber, because a 13th-century window survives at the north end of its basement. About 1571 the apartment range was renovated for Leicester. The veneer of the new masonry on the outside of the building is visible at the junction with the bay window in the great hall. The foundations of two Elizabethan bay windows survive between the hall and the oriel.

THE ORIEL

1 Entrance from the inner court

2 14th-century window tracery lighting the first-floor lobby

3 Frame of a great chamber window

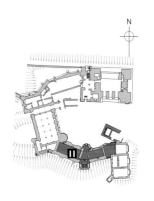

Interior

The visitor should now enter the range through the door of the oriel. This room is remarkable for its date in providing a direct link from the court to the heart of the private chambers, an idea derived from the 'La Rose' Tower in Edward III's lodgings at Windsor. A spiral staircase once led up to the first-floor 'hall place', which acted as a lobby connecting the two main chambers. From the lobby another spiral stair went up in Gaunt's Tower.

No documentation exists for the precise usage of the apartments in Gaunt's time, but it is likely that the great chamber was his audience chamber and also where the most important members of the household staff usually dined. The second chamber was probably his dining room, and beyond this would have been the state bedchamber. Gaunt's Tower provided the duke with his most private rooms – somewhere he might relax and perhaps admire the view. By the time of Queen Elizabeth's visits in the 1570s, the second chamber had become the audience ('presence') chamber, dining took place in the privy chamber and the state bedroom had moved into the new Leicester's Building.

The ground floor of the great chamber probably housed the wardrobe, which included precious possessions such as plate, tapestries and bed-hangings. According to William Oke, Gaunt's clerk of the wardrobe, the duke possessed 'a finer wardrobe than any other Christian king'. Beneath Gaunt's Tower the substantial latrines for the household staff are still visible. The ground floor of the second chamber appears to have been the location of a second privy kitchen listed in 1563, in an ideal location to serve food directly to the apartments above. Previously food might have been brought across the courtyard from the main privy kitchen, via the private door in the oriel.

Down the modern wooden steps is the basement of the privy chamber. By the time of the 1563 survey, beyond the privy chamber were another five chambers grouped around 'the king's chamber with a fair compass window of stone'. Leicester's accommodation was probably in this area during Elizabeth's visits. The survey also appears to place 'the nursery' together with a chamber that 'sometime was the chapel' in this part of the court. Practically none of this can be identified on site now, because most of these rooms were in the lost King Henry's Lodgings. However, the stone foundations thought to belong to the chapel are still visible.

Above: A detail of an 18th-century painting, by Paul Sandby, of Edward III's royal lodgings at Windsor, showing the 'La Rose' Tower (left), the model for the oriel at Kenilworth

Left: A late 15th-century Flemish manuscript depicting John of Gaunt (left) dining with the king of Portugal (centre), in a great chamber with serving hatch and musicians' gallery. John's daughter, Philippa, married King John I of Portugal

12 LEICESTER'S BUILDING

From the privy chamber site, there is a good view into the northern rooms of Leicester's Building. This tower block was erected in 1571 specifically to provide private accommodation for Elizabeth I and her close servants. Elizabeth used it in 1572, and it was subsequently improved for her visit of 1575. To make enough space for a building which is the size of a compact country house, it was extended beyond the medieval curtain wall, the foundations of which run diagonally across the privy chamber site. At full height it was a four-storey building, but because it descends downhill and out over the former ditch, two of the floors – the ground floor and basement – were below the principal floor level.

Interior: the North Wing

The north wing was a direct continuation of the state apartments range and was limited to three floors. On the top floor was the privy chamber, denoted by the apertures for doors and fireplaces surviving in the south wall. The far door led into Elizabeth's withdrawing chamber. The adjacent (eastern) fireplace was added when this space was divided into two rooms to improve the facilities for Elizabeth's visit in 1575.

Exterior

Visitors should now go back into the inner court and proceed clockwise right around the exterior of Leicester's Building. On the north elevation are the vertical scars for the connecting walls to the lost east range. The toothings of the left scar include reused medieval worked stones from a dissolved monastery, possibly Kenilworth Priory.

The east elevation must have presented a splendidly ordered composition, which expressed the functions of its various parts. First, the principal floor is indicated right across the façade by the tallest windows. Second, the right (north) bay of the façade is wider, denoting the state apartments range. Third, the block containing the royal chambers in the left and centre bays is signified by an extra storey.

Continue around the south side of the building, past the projecting (south-west) turret, to face the west elevation. More windows survive on this façade, including the double-transomed windows of the principal floor, to give the best

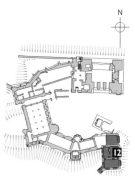

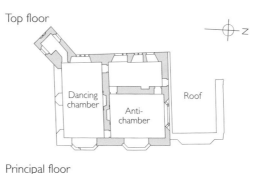
Top floor

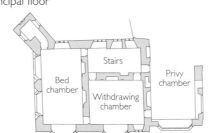
Principal floor

Ground floor

Basement

Above: The great chamber of Hardwick Hall, Derbyshire (1590–7) has a tall plaster frieze similar to ones which existed in the principal chambers of Leicester's Building
Below: Holes for wooden dowels in the east withdrawing chamber in Leicester's Building, to secure the plaster frieze

Facing page: The east elevation of Leicester's Building. The windows of the principal floor occupied by Elizabeth I were destroyed after 1650

Elizabeth and Leicester: the 1575 Visit

Elizabeth's 19-day visit to Kenilworth in 1575 was her longest stay at a courtier's house during any progress

Queen Elizabeth I enjoyed travel and made summer progresses away from London virtually every year in the first half of her reign. She had come to Kenilworth on three previous occasions before her 19-day visit between 9 and 27 July 1575, the longest stay at a courtier's house during any progress. The events can be reconstructed on a daily basis from a long letter by Robert Laneham, and from an account of the festivities by George Gascoigne. Laneham was keeper of the council chamber door, and Gascoigne was a poet and actor commissioned by Leicester to write and organise many of the entertainments.

Leicester hoped to tempt Elizabeth into marriage. Their courtship had been ongoing since 1559. The entertainments included episodes apparently designed to press Leicester's matrimonial suit. A hint of this agenda is contained in the Lady of the Lake's speech to Elizabeth on her arrival: 'The Lake, the Lodge, the Lord [Leicester] are yours to command'. Two days later, as Elizabeth was returning from hunting, she was confronted by a 'savage man' covered in moss and ivy. He learns of the gifts given

to Elizabeth, and in a poetic dialogue with the nymph, Echo, he reveals that these 'tokens of true love' were given by Dudley.

The most pointed reference was to have been Gascoigne's masque 'Zabeta', a play on the name 'Elizabeth'. The story hinged on a debate about whether the chaste nymph, Zabeta, should wed and concluded with a speech urging the queen to marry. However, it was cancelled, ostensibly because of bad weather. Not to be outdone Gascoigne improvised a farewell to the queen, where she was intercepted by 'deep desire' (an actor dressed as a prickly hollybush, representing Leicester), who urged:

> Live here, good Queen, live here; you are
> amongst your friends.
> Their comfort comes when you approach,
> and when you part it ends.

Although she remained on the best of terms with Leicester, Elizabeth never returned to Kenilworth. In 1578 he went on to marry Lettice Knollys, countess of Essex.

Right: Drawings made in 1575 by the Italian artist, Federico Zuccaro, of Robert Dudley, earl of Leicester and Queen Elizabeth I. These are preliminary studies for two complementary portraits of the queen and her favourite courtier specially commissioned by Leicester for the Kenilworth festivities of 1575

impression of grids of fragile tracery set into seemingly paper-thin walls. As Robert Laneham noted in 1575: 'in daytime on every side so glittering by glass; at nights, by continual brightness of candle, fire and torchlight, transparent through the lightsome windows'.

The south-west turret must have been added between 1572 and 1575 to provide the queen with a private stair between the upper floors. Large cracks in the masonry of the south elevation indicate that the entire building threatened to collapse during the turret's construction.

Interior: the Private Rooms

The visitor should now go through the west door into the basement. All the floors were removed after 1650, so the rooms occupied by Elizabeth have to be viewed today from two floors below. The layout of the south rooms can be best understood by studying the internal north wall. The two large fireplaces on the principal (second) floor heated the two inner chambers of Elizabeth's three-room suite, which was entered through the right-hand (east) door from her withdrawing chamber in the east rooms. The fireplace surrounds would have incorporated stones such as marble and alabaster. A wooden partition wall between the two south chambers has been lost. Elizabeth's bedroom almost certainly occupied the right-hand chamber. The left-hand chamber was another withdrawing chamber, and both these rooms enjoyed superb views across the mere.

On the top floor, the single, larger chamber would have been particularly appropriate as the queen's dancing chamber. It was probably beneath the east window of this chamber that the Coventry men performed their play in the outer court on 17 July 1575. Elizabeth saw little of the play because she was distracted by the 'delectable dancing' within the chamber.

Below these rooms, the ground (first) floor was also residential, but it must have been of a lesser status, as it had a fireplace surround carved from the local sandstone. The likely occupants of the ground floor were Elizabeth's ladies. The basement rooms are clearly designed for storage, presumably for the bulkier items of her prodigious travelling wardrobe.

Now proceed through the door in the north-east (right-hand) corner into the basement of the

east rooms. Within this vertiginous space, the principal floor was the withdrawing chamber, the first room of Elizabeth's suite, and the top floor formed an anteroom to the dancing chamber. The physical evidence for original fittings and for the hierarchy of accommodation is especially well preserved on the internal walls of these rooms. For example, rows of small holes (for wooden pegs) on the south and west walls of the principal floor indicate that the queen's withdrawing chamber had a tall plaster frieze.

Return to the south basement and go through the far right-hand (north-west) door into the west basement. This space encompassed the service requirements for the building. A chute for sewage and waste water is built into the east wall; it drained into a culvert beneath the basement floor. It was originally accessed from timber-framed closets on each floor. A fine wooden staircase on a square newel plan must have existed in the southern part of the space to connect the upper floors. Without it, there would have been no direct link between these levels before the south-west turret stair was added.

THE SOUTH ROOMS OF LEICESTER'S BUILDING

1 Doors into the south-west staircase turret

2 West windows reduced to three lights in width to accommodate the addition of the turret

3 Elizabeth's bedroom and withdrawing chamber on the principal floor

4 Elizabeth's dancing chamber on the top floor

13 LEICESTER'S GATEHOUSE

Visitors should now retrace their route out of Leicester's Building, and across the outer court to stand in front of the porch of Leicester's Gatehouse.

Exterior

This was built by Leicester as a gatehouse between 1570 and 1575, and was subsequently converted into a substantial house after 1650. It provided a grand new entrance to the castle from Coventry and Kenilworth parish church. It also gave access to the hunting in the chase by way of a wooden bridge, 600 feet (183m) long, across the north arm of the mere. There must, however, have been a northern entry to the castle since the 12th century, and the 1563 survey records a 'fair gatehouse of stone with a portcullis, going into the town, much in decay'.

As built by Leicester, the gatehouse straddled the medieval curtain wall (removed in 1650), and featured an entrance passage wide enough for carriages at ground level and two floors of lodgings above (see page 46). The corner turrets were originally battlemented. The front pair had porter's lodges and the south-west turret (to the right of the porch) contains a spiral stair to the upper floors. The building follows in the tradition of great medieval gatehouses, perpetuated in Tudor times as symbolic rather than defensive structures. The passage was secured only by a pair of gates and both façades make extensive use of large windows.

The combination of architectural details – the classical plinth and the Tudor Gothic door frames – creates a distinctive style, echoed in Leicester's Building, which suggests that the gatehouse was

built at around the same time. Gothic door frames were still in use in the Elizabethan period, but their selection here was probably a conscious reference to the castle's medieval past.

To convert the gatehouse into a residence for Colonel Hawkesworth, a domestic extension was added on the east side. In addition, the passage was blocked to create a ground floor and basement, and the west porch was added as a new entrance. All the materials were obtained by demolishing Leicester's works elsewhere in the castle, so that the modifications are hardly perceptible. The elaborate classical frontispiece of the porch displays the initials 'R L', for Robert, earl of Leicester, and variations of his badges were worked into the architectural decoration. It takes the form of a triumphal arch and probably originally graced one of the doorways in the inner court buildings, such as the entrance to the forebuilding.

Interior

Through the porch is the ground floor of the gatehouse. The southern room, approached through the wooden screen to the right, contains Elizabethan panelling and a fine alabaster fireplace. These were relocated here after 1650, and give the best impression today of the Elizabethan fittings in the apartments of the castle. The

fireplace probably comes from the privy chamber. It bears Leicester's initials 'R L', with the date '1571', and the motto and badges of the Order of the Garter, of which he was a knight. The floridly carved wooden overmantel has 'E' and 'R' ('Elizabeth Regina') on its bottom cornice and the oak panelling around the room is carved with Leicester's ragged staff device (see page 47).

From the northern room, a doorway leads through into Hawkesworth's 17th-century extension. This provided a kitchen in the basement, additional accommodation and a main staircase. The woodwork of the staircase may come from elsewhere in the castle.

On the first floor the oak panelling in the south room gives an impression of the interior when it was used as a house. The gatehouse proper at this level retains its form as a two-room suite of Elizabethan lodgings over the gate.

The second floor, reached via the wooden spiral stairs, was originally another two-room suite of lodgings, subsequently made into one space. The small rooms in the turrets were retiring rooms or bedrooms. The roof structure, with king-post trusses, was rebuilt in the mid-18th century. This room was used as the council chamber of Kenilworth Town Council from 1958 until recently, and it now houses an exhibition on the theme of 'Leicester and Elizabeth'.

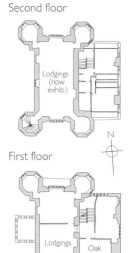

Second floor

First floor

Ground floor

0   5m   0   15ft

Left: The southern room of the gatehouse, with the Elizabethan fireplace and wooden fittings from elsewhere in the castle

Facing page, top: Leicester's Gatehouse, seen from the outer court, with Hawkesworth's extension on the right
Bottom left: The classical frontispiece of the porch, with Leicester's initials 'R L'
Bottom right: The date '1571' on the ground-floor fireplace

⊞ STABLE

From the gatehouse, the visitor should take the path downhill to arrive in front of the stable. A stable is documented at the castle from at least the early 14th century, but the present building was probably erected between 1549 and 1553. The 1563 survey assigns the stable to Leicester's father, John Dudley, earl of Northumberland – 'a very fair and a strong new stable which my lord's grace your father made … in length 180 feet and in breadth 21 feet'. It remains an outstanding survival from a period when grand stable buildings were becoming the fashion. From 1650 until the Victorian period, the building continued in use as a stable and barn, as part of the farm established in the bottom end of the outer court.

The ground floor is built of good ashlar stone against the earlier curtain wall. Its original features include the porch, two doorways to the north and the windows (the larger ones were modified later). The large south entrance was rebuilt in brick in the early 19th century. The upper storey is of timber-framed construction, with decorative square panelling along the west face, which was restored in the 1970s. The ornamental timber braces are specifically in the form of ragged staves, the Beauchamp device adopted by Northumberland and Leicester. The stable building takes on further significance when we remember that both men were Masters of the Horse to Edward VI and Elizabeth I respectively.

Inside the stable, the impressive open roof of eleven bays is essentially contemporary with the erection of the building. In the 1563 survey, the stable is described as having '30 rooms [stalls] for great horses besides rooms for 20 geldings'. The northern bays were still fitted with stalls and in use as a stable in the mid-Victorian period. Other details of the building's original usage are less easy to reconstruct. Initially, there was an upper floor for storage, and perhaps for accommodation for grooms. The 1563 survey notes that if the stable was 'boarded over the joists', in it 'might be laid 300 loads of hay'. During the 1930s, 'Lord Leicester's Barn Restaurant' operated in the southern half of the building – a space occupied today by an introductory exhibition to the castle.

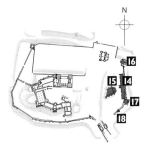

OUTER COURT

15 Collegiate Chapel

In front of the stable lie the foundations of a collegiate chapel built for Thomas of Lancaster between about 1314 and 1322. It was one of the largest private chapels of its time, about 45 feet (14m) high and at least 100 feet (30m) long. Its west end is now buried under the later bank. It was possibly demolished about 1524, when the foundations might have been reused for a timber-framed building brought from the Pleasance. This, in turn, was probably removed by Leicester. The only recognisable features of the foundations are the polygonal apse for the chapel's altar, and fragments of a reset sedilia, the seating for priests officiating at the Mass.

16 Lunn's Tower

To the north of the stable is Lunn's Tower, the best preserved of King John's wall towers of about 1210–15. The ground floor was powerfully equipped with five fish-tailed arrowloops, but the two remaining today have been restored, and are best seen from the exterior. The external stair turret gave access to the two upper floors and the wall-walk. The second floor was built as a residential chamber, and the first floor was subsequently converted into a chamber as well. A two-storey timber building was once connected to the tower. It was probably the house built by the constable, John Ashford, which in 1400 was confirmed in the possession of his wife, together with 'the tower adjoining'.

17 Water Tower

To the south of the stable is the Water Tower, so-called because it overlooked the lower pool. It was probably built by Thomas of Lancaster in the early 14th century. Its exterior has pyramidal corner buttresses and cruciform arrowloops with oillets (or eyelets), characteristic of the period. The tower provided additional lodgings for Thomas's leading retainers. The ground-floor door led into a private chamber with a fireplace and latrine. An internal spiral stair gave access to a superior first-floor chamber, which has two-light windows with built-in seats. The rows of holes cut into the interior walls relate to its use as a 'pigeon house', as documented in 1748.

18 Outer Curtain Wall

The surviving length of the outer curtain wall, which runs towards Mortimer's Tower, retains features indicating the former existence of buildings adjacent to the wall. A residential chamber in the thickness of the wall is equipped with a latrine and a fireplace, probably dating from the early 14th century. The 1563 survey also records a brewhouse, water mill and bakehouse in this area of the outer bailey.

Top left: The exterior of Lunn's Tower, commanding the north-east corner of the outer curtain. On the ground floor is a Victorian restoration of a fish-tailed arrowloop, and at the top left is a latrine chamber discharging into the moat

Top right: The Water Tower, added to the outer curtain in the early 14th century, with a pyramidal corner buttress (left) and a ground-floor latrine chamber (right). The large ground-floor aperture is a later modification

WATER TOWER
First floor

Ground floor

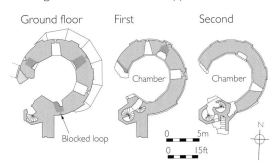

Ground floor   First   Second

Chamber   Chamber

Blocked loop

0   5m

0   15ft

The Elizabethan Garden

The gardens at Kenilworth drew inspiration from French and Italian Renaissance gardens, such as the famous Tivoli gardens near Rome

During Queen Elizabeth I's reign, pleasure gardens became an essential accessory of the great courtier house. The 1575 garden is the first of her reign for which we have detailed evidence, thanks to the eyewitness account by Robert Laneham. The garden evidently drew inspiration from French and Italian Renaissance models, such as the famous Tivoli gardens at the Villa d'Este near Rome (laid out in the 1550s). It was a privy garden for the queen's use, because Laneham tells us that he gained access one day when 'the garden door was open and her highness out hunting'. He saw the spectacular centrepiece, the white marble fountain with two Atlas figures carrying a sphere from which water cascaded down. Sudden spouts of water could be contrived 'at the twist of a stopcock' to soak any unfortunate spectator 'found hot in desire'.

The four quarters of the garden were divided by walks of grass edged with sand, and planted with herbs, flowers and 'fruit trees bedecked with their apples, pears and ripe cherries' – a remarkable combination for mid-July. In the centre of each bed stood an obelisk 15 feet (4.6m) high, an ancient symbol of rulership, said, improbably, to have been carved from Egyptian porphyry. The garden was viewed from a grassy terrace on the south side and from leafy arbours on the east and west, with an elaborate aviary in classical style to the north, filled with song-birds. The use of a terrace, an aviary and obelisks is the first recorded appearance of these Italianate features in an English garden. In placing his garden within the walls of a medieval castle, Leicester was following French Renaissance precedents, like the château at Amboise which he saw as a young man. However, this might not have been the first garden in the outer bailey. Previous gardens are mentioned in medieval accounts, and possibly the 'garden at the jousting-place' noted in 1463 was on this site.

Above: A garden depicted in a tapestry made for the earl of Leicester about 1585

🇮🇪 OUTER COURT AND GARDEN

The 1563 survey divides the outer court into three areas: the 'base court', the 'court at the left hand' and the 'court of the right hand'. These divisions are still visible, with the gate to the left court adjacent to Leicester's Building and with the right court largely occupied by the garden. Their former existence emphasises the structured layout of the castle plan, with the more public activities taking place in the base court, and the more private areas grouped in the left and right courts.

To follow this tour, start at the gap between Leicester's Building and the outer line of walls. Ahead are the remains of the wall with the gate to the left court. On entering the court, the dominant feature immediately to the right is the multi-faceted exterior of Gaunt's Tower, rising from a basement which houses the cess-pit for its latrines. Beyond it is the base of the splendid 'compass' window, which lit the high end of the Elizabethan great chamber, supported on a restored buttress. Proceed to the far end of the court, then look back to the west elevation of the great hall, flanked by the Strong and Saintlowe towers; the symmetry and verticality of Gaunt's building can be appreciated from here.

The mound in front of the great hall was a pre-existing feature, which was heightened at some time after the hall was built, perhaps as a terrace for watching entertainments on the mere. To the right (north) of the water gate is the best length of wall to preserve window and fireplace apertures of various dates – testimony to the domestic buildings once contained in the left court. The 1545 survey states that 'about the walls there be houses builded for 200 persons to lodge in'.

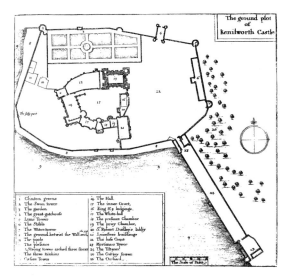

Visitors should proceed through the arch in the dividing wall between the courts, to reach the site of the Pleasance buildings. Dugdale's plan of 1656, above, locates the Pleasance buildings against the north face of the wall, where apertures for fireplaces are still visible.

Further north along the outer curtain wall is the so-called King's Gate, an entrance introduced at some date after 1650 for agricultural use, but reusing medieval stones. The Swan Tower sits at the north-west corner of the curtain wall, already called 'le Swannesnest' in 1439–40 and presumably so named because of swans on the mere. It was probably built in the later 14th century but little survives above basement level. Elizabethan details in the stonework suggest that it was converted into a banqueting house by Leicester, perhaps as an adjunct to the garden.

The path up the steps and through the Swan Tower leads to the site of the Elizabethan Garden. This was the first great garden of Elizabeth's reign for which a detailed contemporary description exists. Practically nothing survived after the mid-17th century, when the outer curtain wall was destroyed and replaced by the existing wall on a different alignment. On the south side, the terrace and the restored entrance from the forebuilding can still be appreciated. The site was subsequently cultivated as a kitchen garden and orchard until the mid-20th century.

A Tudor garden was replanted here in 1975, based on Dugdale's plan of 1656. Currently a programme of archaeological investigation is taking place, in advance of a more authentic reconstruction of the Tudor garden. The most significant discovery to date has been the foundations of a fountain, the central feature of the garden, on an axis with the approach from the forebuilding.

Left: A plan of the castle, published in 1656 by Sir William Dugdale. The garden site is shown (top) and all the main buildings are named (bottom)

Below: View of Kenilworth Castle, about 1830, by J M W Turner. For the same view today, see page 2

Facing page: The base of the Elizabethan 'compass' window in the great chamber, overlooking the site of the mere

History

The first castle at Kenilworth was constructed in the early 1120s. By the 1170s Kenilworth was judged to be of such strategic importance that it was taken into royal control. It was strengthened by King Henry II and King John, and it withstood a full-scale siege in 1266. The castle's residential accommodation was enlarged by John of Gaunt in the late 14th century. Two hundred years later, Robert Dudley remodelled Kenilworth for Queen Elizabeth I's visits in 1572 and 1575. The castle was slighted after the Civil War and fell into ruin.

READING THE HISTORY

This section describes the history of the castle from its construction by Geoffrey de Clinton, through to its heyday during the Tudor period, and its later abandonment as a major residence.

THE DE CLINTONS: 1120–74

Geoffrey de Clinton established the first castle on this site at Kenilworth (Chinewrde) in the early 1120s. Geoffrey was chamberlain and treasurer to King Henry I (1100–35), on whose support he depended entirely for his advancement. Henry had suspicions in 1119 about the loyalty of Roger, the new earl of Warwick (1119–53), and so he promoted Geoffrey in Warwickshire to counter Roger's influence. Geoffrey held the royal post of sheriff by 1121, and by 1124 he was established as a great magnate in the county. He was granted lands in the royal manor of Stoneleigh, on one part of which he established Kenilworth Castle and on the other, downstream from the castle, he founded Kenilworth Priory in or before 1124.

It has been speculated that Geoffrey's castle was only a motte of earth crowned by timber buildings. Yet a strong case can be made to show that the existing stone keep must have been constructed in the favourable circumstances directly after 1124. An undertaking on this scale could not have been achieved without royal resources, and in these years Geoffrey enjoyed the undiminished favour of King Henry. In 1130, however, his relationship with the king began to

sour. At Geoffrey's death, about 1133, his son and successor, Geoffrey II, was a minor, and by then the power of Roger, earl of Warwick, was in the ascendant in Warwickshire. Geoffrey II and his uncle, William de Clinton, came to an accommodation with the earl, which included Geoffrey's marriage to his infant daughter, Agnes. His independence was weakened further from 1135, following the accession of King Stephen (1135–54), and the beginnings of civil war in England. During his career, Geoffrey II never commanded the resources to undertake major works at Kenilworth or at the other De Clinton castle of Brandon near Coventry.

Above: The coffins reputed to be those of Geoffrey de Clinton and his son, excavated in the chapter house of Kenilworth Priory about 1925

Left: Reconstruction of De Clinton's castle as it might have appeared about 1190, after some modifications made in King Henry II's reign

Facing page: Detail from a painting of 1862 by the local artist, Thomas Baker, entitled Lord Leycester Tower, *but actually showing the Saintlowe Tower, overgrown with ivy*

Kenilworth Priory

Kenilworth Priory was established by Geoffrey de Clinton at the same time as the castle

The priory of St Mary was as integral a part of the medieval landscape of Kenilworth as the castle, but its suppression in 1538 has removed its physical traces far more completely. Its few remains lie 600 yards (0.5km) from the castle, in 'Abbey Fields' (the priory was raised to abbey status in 1447). The two structures still standing are part of the impressive gatehouse (1361–75), and the so-called 'barn' which today displays archaeological fragments from the priory. Parts of the cruciform church can also be traced, and the lake in Abbey Fields is on part of the site of the medieval fishponds.

The priory was a monastery for Augustinian canons established by Geoffrey de Clinton about 1124, at the same time as the castle. The associated foundation of a castle with an Augustinian priory was fashionable among the courtiers of King Henry I. The Augustinian canons were popular with aristocratic patrons because they could render useful services beyond the cloister, a facility exploited by the lords of Kenilworth. They expected hospitality at the priory and the priors became in effect their local agents. In 1380 the prior served as the clerk of works at the castle. In June 1372, John of Gaunt ordered the priory to lay in stocks of good wine for an intended visit, and in November 1379 he ordered the relaying of the great chamber floor at the priory for dancing at Christmas. These impositions were materially worthwhile for the priory, even if spiritually questionable. The priory was well endowed with lands and had the second highest income of any monastery in Warwickshire at the suppression. Ironically, in the mid-16th century materials from its redundant buildings were reused in works at the castle.

Right: The west door of St Nicholas's parish church, Kenilworth, is a remarkable assemblage of Romanesque carved stones reused from the adjacent priory after the suppression of 1538

Below: The priory ruins as they appeared in 1729 in an engraving by Samuel and Nathaniel Buck, showing the chapter house wall (left) and the 'barn' and ruined gatehouse (right)

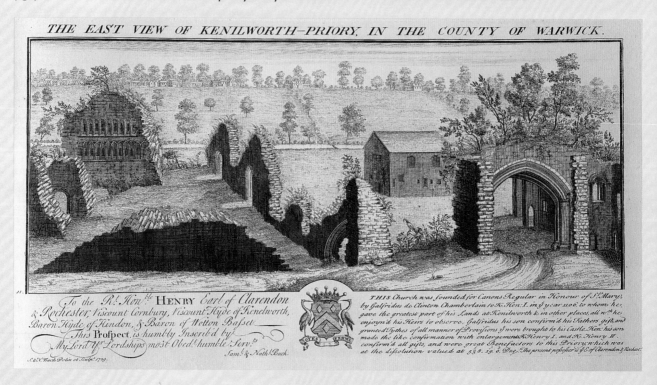

THE EAST VIEW OF KENILWORTH-PRIORY, IN THE COUNTY OF WARWICK.

Brandon Castle provides an important clue that the keep at Kenilworth should be attributed to De Clinton patronage. Its distinctive plan, with projecting angle turrets and prominent intermediate buttresses, is reflected on a smaller scale in the stone keep at Brandon, excavated in 1947. No independent dating evidence survives for Brandon, but a castle was in existence there by the time Geoffrey II married Agnes of Warwick, and it would be surprising if keeps of related design, in two castles possessed by Geoffrey I, were not both commissioned during his lifetime.

THE CROWN: 1174–1244

Kenilworth Castle was garrisoned for King Henry II (1154–89) during the 'great rebellion' of his son in 1173–4. At about the same time, Geoffrey II de Clinton died. The castle was then judged to be of such strategic importance that the king took it into royal control. At this time the castle consisted of at least the stone keep with its forebuilding, and a single bailey approached by a causeway across a lake. During the next 70 years, the castle's fortifications assumed the extent and form we see today: the outer circuit of stone walls with towers, and the dam with its outworks to control the water defences.

One result of royal ownership was that the history of the castle was to become better documented, especially through the annual returns (Pipe Rolls) of the sheriff to the exchequer. For example, we learn of the existence of a king's great chamber, a king's chapel and a queen's chamber in records of 1234–5 and 1241. By then, the defences had been largely completed, but the accounts are less helpful about these works. Parallels with castle-building elsewhere, however, suggest that they were mainly commissioned by Henry II, between about 1184 and 1189, and by King John. The latter spent the large sum of about £1,100 on Kenilworth, mostly between 1210 and 1215, as part of a campaign to strengthen major royal castles following the papal Interdict of 1208, and his own excommunication.

The stone walls of the inner bailey date from no later than Henry II's reign, and the same is probably true of the simple stone gatehouse later incorporated into Mortimer's Tower. The presence of a gatehouse in this position must indicate the existence of an outer bailey, probably defended by

a bank and ditch. King John's reign is the most likely time when the outer bailey received its present circuit of stone walls with towers. The best surviving examples are Lunn's Tower and Mortimer's Tower. The latter is an early example of a twin-towered gatehouse. As part of the same programme of extending the fortifications, the dam was heightened to enlarge the mere. Within the castle, substantial improvements were made to the keep and a small barbican was probably added to protect the inner bailey gate.

In the end, the strength of John's castles availed him little, in the face of his unpleasant personality and an inability to manage the great barons. In 1215, he was forced to sign the Magna Carta. When John died in 1216, the French prince, Louis, invaded England in support of the rebel barons. Nevertheless, it was the strength of another castle, Dover, which thwarted Louis' campaign, and John's young son inherited successfully as King Henry III (1216–72).

Above left: Another early example of a twin-towered gatehouse like Mortimer's Tower at Kenilworth was King John's gatehouse at Dover Castle, shown here in a reconstruction of the French siege of Dover in 1216
Above: One of the fish-tailed arrowloops for use by crossbows – part of King John's additions to the top of the keep
Left: The tomb effigy of King John in the choir of Worcester Cathedral, supported by representations of the local saints Oswald and Wulfstan, carved about 1230

SIMON DE MONTFORT: 1244–65

Born in France about 1208, Simon de Montfort was a landless younger son of noble birth. It suited Henry III to promote him because of his predisposition towards French favourites. Simon's father, also Simon de Montfort (about 1170–1218), was the famous French crusader who had campaigned against the Albigensian heretics in southern France. From his father, the younger Simon inherited his military ability, piety and sense of moral duty, tempered by more than a degree of self-interest. His fortunes rose rapidly after his arrival in England in 1230. He married Eleanor, the king's sister, in 1238 and was created earl of Leicester in 1239, thus regaining his family's former English estates.

In 1244, Simon was given custody of Kenilworth Castle, and was granted it for life in 1253. It was already an exceptional fortress, but he is reported to have strengthened it further. The chronicler refers to 'unheard of … machines' at the castle, probably the trebuchets which were to play a significant role in the siege of 1266. He might also have been responsible for completing the scheme of defence originally conceived by King John, by creating the Brays, the large outwork crucial to the security of the dam.

The turning-point in Simon's life came in 1258, when he headed the confederacy of reforming barons against King Henry III – a fateful decision which led ultimately to his defeat and death at the hands of royal forces at the battle of Evesham in 1265. After Evesham, some of his followers made a last stand at Kenilworth, enduring the longest siege in English medieval history until surrendering to the king in December 1266.

Above: Caerphilly Castle, south Wales, built 1268–71 for Gilbert II de Clare, earl of Gloucester, has water defences like Kenilworth's. Gilbert was with the royal forces at the siege of Kenilworth in 1266, and the strength of its defences made a lasting impression on him

Below: *The death and mutilation of Simon de Montfort at the battle of Evesham, from an early 14th-century manuscript*

The Great Siege of 1266

The siege of Kenilworth Castle by royal forces in 1266 was one of the few full-scale medieval sieges on English soil. A full array of the latest weaponry was pitted against a formidable modern fortress, in a type of warfare developed by the crusaders in the Near East.

Simon de Montfort had been killed at Evesham on 4 August 1265. In January 1266 his eldest son, Simon the younger, promised to surrender Kenilworth to the king, but his father's supporters inside refused. King Henry III's patience finally snapped after his messenger returned with a severed hand. An all-out siege began on 21 June 1266, with the garrison now commanded by Henry, 7th baron Hastings (d.1268), an outstanding leader who would maintain the defenders' morale through great deprivation during the next six months.

The royal forces set up stone-throwing machines to the north, facing the keep, and to the south across the mere. However, they were thwarted by

the superior range of weaponry inside and the king had to send to London for larger machines. The most devastating siege weapon of the day was the trebuchet, capable of hurling stone balls weighing up to 300 lbs (140kg) with remarkable accuracy. In 1960, archaeologists excavated such missiles in the outer bailey, which had been catapulted 350 yards (320m) across the mere and had violently destroyed a building inside the wall. The water defences prevented the undermining of the castle walls, so the king even brought barges from Chester for an abortive assault across the mere. A parliament held by King Henry near the castle, perhaps on the land now called 'Parliament Piece', resulted in the Dictum of Kenilworth, which would permit the rebels to regain forfeited lands on payment of heavy fines. Eventually, disease and starvation brought about what the assault had failed to deliver, and the remnants of the garrison surrendered on these favourable terms on 14 December 1266.

The siege of Kenilworth Castle was one of the few full-scale medieval sieges on English soil

Left: Stone balls being hurled at a castle by a 'perrier', a simple form of siege engine operated by a counterpoise like the larger trebuchets used at Kenilworth in 1266; from a French manuscript of about 1340

THE HOUSE OF LANCASTER: 1266–1361

Immediately after the surrender, Henry III granted Kenilworth to his younger son, Edmund (1245–96), created earl of Lancaster in 1267. Thus began almost 200 years of ownership by the house of Lancaster, who were successively earls, dukes and kings, and were responsible for the distinctive development of the castle as a palace. In 1279 it was the setting for an Arthurian 'round table', a series of tournaments and festivities based on medieval romance literature, very fashionable among the elite of European chivalry. The celebrations were attended by 100 knights and their ladies, and the main guest was King Edward I, Edmund of Lancaster's brother. He was there to acknowledge the farewell to arms of his close friend, Roger Mortimer. At the tournament, which may have been held on the Brays, Mortimer won the prize of a gold lion.

Edmund's son, Thomas (about 1278–1322), received a grant of his father's lands in 1298. Thomas of Lancaster entertained on a scale rivalling that of the king and maintained a household of

Right: The Lady Chapel of Lichfield Cathedral (built about 1320) provides a good impression of the interior of the collegiate chapel of St Mary at Kenilworth, built by the master mason Richard de Thwaites, with a polygonal apse beyond the altar

Below: A reconstruction of Kenilworth Castle as it might have appeared just before the siege of 1266. An outer circuit of stone walls has been added, the dam has been raised to hold back the large mere and the outwork of the Brays has been constructed

over 500 retainers. At Kenilworth he created a deer park of 800 acres (324ha) and probably added the Water Tower to provide additional accommodation for his leading retainers. Furthermore, between about 1314 and 1322, a new collegiate chapel dedicated to St Mary was constructed in the outer bailey of the castle. Collegiate foundations on a large scale were fashionable acts of late medieval piety, of which the most famous example was King Edward III's foundation of St George's, Windsor (1348). Thomas planned his foundation for 13 secular priests, but he did not live long enough to establish the college and nothing more is heard of it. When he entered into open rebellion against King Edward II (1307–27), the castle was taken into royal custody, and Thomas was executed in 1322 after the battle of Boroughbridge.

However, Edward II's reassertion of power was short-lived and ironically it was Thomas's younger brother, Henry, who captured Edward II in south Wales and brought him back to Kenilworth in 1326, where he was forced to abdicate. The estates of

Lancaster, including Kenilworth Castle, were formally restored to Henry in 1327. At his death in 1345 he was succeeded by his son, Henry of Grosmont (about 1300–61), who was a comrade-in-arms of King Edward III in his wars in Flanders, France and Scotland. He was a founder knight of Edward's Order of the Garter and was created duke of Lancaster in 1351. At Kenilworth he evidently remodelled the great hall. The contract of 1347 indicates that the hall was the same size as the existing great hall, providing a valuable insight into the scale of the castle's accommodation before the works of Henry's son-in-law, John of Gaunt.

Left: The effigy of Edmund, earl of Lancaster, the first member of the house of Lancaster to own Kenilworth Castle, from his tomb in Westminster Abbey (1296)

JOHN OF GAUNT: 1361–99

John of Gaunt was the greatest nobleman in late
medieval England and the most ambitious builder
at Kenilworth since King John. The fourth son of
Edward III, Gaunt was born in 1340 at Ghent in
Flanders. He became the main force in English
government after the premature deaths of his
older brothers. In 1359 he married Blanche of
Lancaster, Duke Henry's younger daughter, and
acquired Kenilworth Castle on her father's death
in 1361. In 1362, Gaunt was created duke of
Lancaster and took possession of his wife's vast
Lancastrian estates. Tragically for Gaunt, Blanche
died in 1368, and in 1371 he entered into a
marriage of political convenience with Constanza,
daughter and heiress of Pedro I, the recently
assassinated king of Castile and León in Spain.
From January 1372, Gaunt titled himself 'king of
Castile and León'.

Thus, from the early 1370s, Gaunt literally
required accommodation fit for a king. It is no
coincidence that major works are recorded at
Kenilworth from about 1373 until 1380. Such
was his wealth that comparable works were
under way simultaneously at several of his
properties, including Hertford Castle and the
Savoy Palace in London, but Kenilworth alone
survives to inform us of the palatial quality of his
architecture. In fact, Gaunt's constant involvement
in national government and expeditions abroad

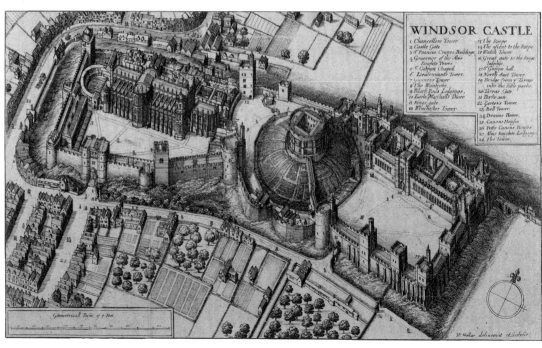

meant that he seldom visited Kenilworth, so perhaps the new work served rather to appease his wife during his flagrant adultery in the 1370s with Katherine Swynford.

The scheme for the new work was modelled on his father's new lodgings at Windsor Castle (1357–68). Both Henry Spenser, the chief mason at Kenilworth, and William Wintringham, Gaunt's master carpenter, had worked previously at Windsor. The core of Gaunt's work was the new great hall, with remodelled apartments, services and kitchens. The most innovative feature of the Windsor lodgings – the unified treatment of its main façade – finds an echo in the finely composed west elevation of the hall between the Saintlowe and Strong towers. Extensive works at Kenilworth are also recorded between 1389 and 1393, under the local mason Robert Skillington, after Gaunt had virtually given up campaigning overseas. The projects under way were apparently of a more practical nature, involving major repairs to walls, gates and bridges, and work on the keep 'for the safeguard of the duke's jewels there'.

Left: John of Gaunt's great hall, with the bay window (centre), seen from the oriel of his state apartments (left)
Below: A reconstruction of Kenilworth Castle as it might have appeared about 1420, with the additions of the collegiate chapel and Water Tower (foreground), Gaunt's remodelling of the inner court (centre) and Henry V's Pleasance (top right)

The Mere and the Pleasance

Kenilworth conjured up the image of a castle of medieval romance, encircled by water

The artificial lake known as the mere, protecting the south and west of Kenilworth Castle, was among the largest medieval, man-made water defences in Britain. A lake must have been created with Geoffrey de Clinton's castle, because a charter of about 1125 permitted the canons of the priory to catch fish in his 'pool' on Thursdays. About 1210 King John substantially enlarged the mere to create a body of water half a mile (800m) long and 500 feet (150m) wide.

The mere and its associated features were not constructed just for military purposes, but were of economic benefit too. The pools supplied fish and wildfowl, and provided the power for water-mills. It was, however, the scenic and recreational qualities which came to be most appreciated. Seen across the mere, Kenilworth conjured up the image of a castle of medieval romance, encircled by water. An Arthurian 'round table' was held here in 1279, and in 1575 Elizabeth I was greeted by the Lady of the Lake 'who had kept this lake since Arthur's days'.

The most extensive of these recreational facilities was 'the Pleasance in the Marsh', built for Henry V. This took the form of a luxurious manor house with gardens surrounded by a double moat with a harbour. The 1563 survey notes that 'in times past [the king] would go in a boat out of the castle to banquet' there, and it was evidently designed for private entertainment. The ultimate source for the Pleasance was the garden-palaces of Islamic Spain and Sicily, as emulated in northern Europe by the romantic castle and park of Count Robert II of Artois at Hesdin (Flanders, about 1300), which included a 'house in the marsh'. The Pleasance was abandoned in Henry VIII's reign and only its earthworks are visible today, standing on private farmland.

Above: This April scene from the Très Riches Heures manuscript of the duke of Berry (about 1415) conjures up an image of the Pleasance at Kenilworth, with a walled garden and belvedere tower (right) looking back over a lake to a castle

Right: View from the Strong Tower of part of the area once occupied by the mere. Purlieu Lane (top right) can be followed on foot to the edge of the site of the Pleasance

THE LANCASTRIAN KINGS AND
THE EARLY TUDORS: 1399–1547

The accession of Henry Bolingbroke, Gaunt's son, as King Henry IV (1399–1413) brought the title and estates of the duchy of Lancaster to the Crown. Kenilworth became a favoured residence of the Lancastrian kings. It was in the great hall in 1414 that Henry V (1413–22) received the insulting gift of tennis balls from the French dauphin, provoking the campaign which led to the famous victory at Agincourt in 1415. Henry VI (1422–71) and his queen were frequently at Kenilworth in the 1450s, as the midlands assumed a key role in the Wars of the Roses. This interest continued after the victory of Henry Tudor at Bosworth Field in 1485. As King Henry VII (1485–1509) he was a regular visitor to the castle, drawn there in part by the importance of the city of Coventry and the pageants of its guilds. He and his wife Elizabeth were admitted as members of the Trinity Guild in 1499. Their son, Henry VIII (1509–47), picked out Kenilworth as one of three 'ancient castles' in the kingdom which he wished to see maintained.

The extent of John of Gaunt's new buildings meant that the works of his successors were primarily concerned with maintenance and repairs. Such additions as were made at the castle relate mainly to the expansion of its facilities for pleasure and relaxation. About 1415 Henry V commissioned 'the Pleasance in the Marsh' out of waste land at the far end of the mere. Maintenance on the garden in the Pleasance is referred to in 1463, and in the same year a 'jousting place' in the midst of a garden in the castle is mentioned. In 1492–3 Henry VII had a tennis court built. In Henry VIII's reign the Pleasance was abandoned and at least one of its buildings – 'a praty banketynge house of tymbre' – was re-erected in the base court of the castle. The east range of the castle's inner court, 'King Henry's Lodgings', was rebuilt in timber between 1530 and 1532, in advance of an impending royal visit. An informative survey of the castle was made at the end of Henry's reign, about 1545. It records the castle's 'fair chambers' with 'great bay windows', 'very commodious to see the deer coursed and the fish taken'. The scene was set for the most extravagant royal entertainment at Kenilworth by Robert Dudley, earl of Leicester.

Left: The Lancastrian kings depicted in the 15th-century stained glass of St Mary's Guildhall, Coventry: Henry IV (left), Henry V (centre), Henry VI (right)

Below: The marriage of King John I of Portugal to Philippa of Lancaster, John of Gaunt's eldest daughter. Their third son was Prince Henry 'the Navigator', the pioneer of Portuguese exploration overseas

IOHAN DUDLEY, Hertogh van Nort humberland onder Eduard den VI.

THE DUDLEY FAMILY:1547–88

John Dudley (about 1504–53) and his fourth son, Robert (1533–88), were granted Kenilworth Castle in 1553 and 1563 respectively. They had a major impact on the buildings we see today. The Dudleys rose to prominence through service to the Tudor monarchy over three generations, and on two occasions might have become kings of England themselves. John Dudley ingratiated himself with Henry VIII through military service to become the dominant force in the reign of Henry's young son, Edward VI (1547–53). John became earl of Warwick in January 1547 and duke of Northumberland in October 1551. His coup to oppose the succession of the Catholic Mary Tudor, by promoting his daughter-in-law, Lady Jane Grey, ended in his execution in August 1553.

The family recovered from this setback, and with the accession of Mary's sister, Queen Elizabeth I (1558–1603), the two surviving sons, Robert and his elder brother Ambrose (d.1590), slowly accrued offices, titles and estates. Robert was the courtier on the most intimate terms with Elizabeth, sharing her passions for riding and dancing. She came close to marrying him after the death in 1560 of his first wife, Amy Robsart, but the established aristocracy fostered suspicion about a new family which had already produced one over-mighty subject.

The Dudleys went to considerable lengths to trace their noble descent, especially from the

Above: John Dudley, duke of Northumberland, from a 16th-century Dutch engraving
Right: Reconstruction of Leicester's Gatehouse, as it appeared from the inner court in 1575, with the outer curtain walls linking to it. See page 28 for a view of the gatehouse today

At Northumberland's execution, Kenilworth returned to the Crown. Ten years later, Elizabeth I renewed the grant to Robert Dudley, and she stayed at Kenilworth four times: in 1566, 1568, 1572 and finally in 1575.

On the one hand, Leicester's new works for her visits of 1572 and 1575 strove to promote the medieval associations of the castle. The Gothic great hall of John of Gaunt was left untouched, and Leicester's new gatehouse was modelled on the Beauchamp gatehouse at Warwick Castle. On the other hand, his work also incorporated the style and luxury of the northern Renaissance, exemplified in large glazed windows, plaster friezes and ceilings, classical fireplaces and a great garden. The castle also housed a collection of about 50 paintings, some of which he had commissioned especially for the 1575 visit. The image of the castle as Renaissance country house appears in French châteaux almost certainly known to Leicester, like Gaillon (1502–10) and Ecouen (1538–55). The idea is found elsewhere in the period, for example at Ludlow and Raglan castles, but the Kenilworth remodelling was the most extensive and remains the best preserved.

Leicester came to appreciate the importance of his midland estates. He visited Kenilworth almost every year after 1570, and in 1571 he founded Lord Leycester's Hospital in Warwick. His remodelling of the castle dates almost entirely from 1570 to 1575, and was subsidised by

Beauchamp earls of Warwick, whose territorial dominance in the midlands both Northumberland and his sons sought to recreate. Ambrose was made earl of Warwick in 1561, and Robert was created earl of Leicester and baron of Denbigh in September 1564. Both brothers, like their father, adopted the Beauchamp device of the bear and ragged staff, with which Robert emblazoned his possessions. The household inventory of Kenilworth Castle in 1588, for example, lists: 'a great bedstead all painted over with crimson, and silvered with roses, four bears and ragged staves, all silvered, standing upon the corners'. The roses refer to the heraldic cinquefoil, trimmed with ermine, denoting the title of earl of Leicester.

Northumberland might have had control of Kenilworth Castle from 1549, the year in which he acquired the dissolved abbey, even though a grant was not made to him until a few months before his death. A survey of the castle made when Robert took possession in 1563 indicates that Northumberland built the existing stable and also probably created the tiltyard in its present form. Similarities of architectural detail between the stable and the forebuilding of the keep raise the possibility that Northumberland was also planning to remodel the keep. Interestingly, he was the patron of the painter and architect John Shute, the author of the first book in English on classical architecture, and he had already remodelled the family castle at Dudley in Staffordshire.

Above left: The château of Ecouen near Paris, one of the most fashionable courtier houses of 16th-century France
Above: The bear and ragged staff device, from Leicester's tomb in St Mary's, Warwick
Below: Lord Leycester's Hospital, Warwick, founded by him in 1571 as an act of local beneficence

'Caesar's tower' (the keep) and the state apartments. Everything was being made ready for a royal visit, which materialised in 1572. The famous privy garden is not recorded until the visit of 1575, but the existence of a garden by 1572 seems probable. Elizabeth never came to Kenilworth again after 1575, but Leicester continued to visit regularly and stipulated in his will that the castle's contents were 'not to be altered or removed', as if to immortalise the events of July 1575.

The significance of the works at Kenilworth for Elizabethan architecture cannot be overstated. The setting of Leicester's Building within a castle with a keep and towers meant that it had to be of extraordinary height, creating the precedent for the 'midland high house', of which Hardwick Hall (1590–7) is the ultimate statement. The brittle, thin walls and grids of windows are the prototypes for the High Elizabethan style of the 1580s and 1590s. The scale of the accommodation also marks out Kenilworth as the first really great prodigy house of Elizabeth's reign, and inspired leading courtiers like Lord Burghley to renovate their existing houses.

substantial land grants from the queen. Letters to Leicester in the summer of 1571 from his architect, William Spicer, indicate extensive works in progress on 'the new tower' (Leicester's Building),

Above: A woodcut from George Turberville's The Noble Arte of Venerie or Hunting, *1575. Elizabeth's favourite recreation at Kenilworth was hunting. The gamekeeper's records include entries such as 'killed by the queen, a bold buck'*

Right: The effigies of Robert Dudley and his third wife, Lettice Knollys, on their tomb in the Beauchamp Chapel at St Mary's church, Warwick

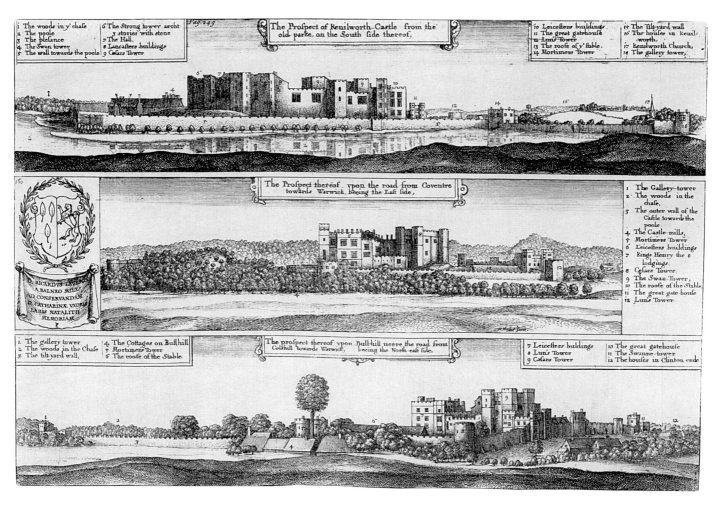

DESTRUCTION – FROM PALACE TO FARMHOUSE: 1588–1800

When Leicester died in 1588 without legitimate male issue, there ensued almost two decades of legal and family wranglings before the castle reverted to the Crown early in the reign of James I (1603–25). In 1612 it was conveyed to Prince Charles, the future King Charles I (1625–49). At his marriage in 1626, the castle was part of the marriage portion of his new queen, Henrietta Maria, and it was held in stewardship for her by Robert Carey, earl of Monmouth (1626–39). The castle was well maintained under the first two Stuart kings, and several royal visits took place, the best-known being that of 1624 when Ben Jonson's *The Masque of Owls* was performed. Visitors noted in 1634 that the state apartments were 'all adorned with fair and rich chimneypieces of alabaster, black marble, and of joiner's work in curious carved wood'.

In October 1642, soon after the beginning of the Civil War, Charles I withdrew the Royalist garrison from Kenilworth after the indecisive battle of Edgehill in October 1642. The castle was then occupied by the Parliamentarians and remained largely unscathed. However, following the uprisings of 1648, prompted by the imprisonment of Charles I, Parliament hardened its attitude to the destruction of all former Royalist strongholds. The ensuing abandonment of castles as major residences was one of the most decisive changes in the history of the English landscape. During 1649 several parliamentary orders were issued for the slighting of Kenilworth, but Henry Carey (d.1661) successfully petitioned 'that it be slighted with as little spoil to the dwelling house [the apartment ranges] as might be'.

In September 1649 the local antiquary, Sir William Dugdale (1605–86), made sketches of the castle, aware that it was about to be slighted. These were engraved and published in 1656 in his *Antiquities of Warwickshire* (see above), together with the first known plan of the castle and a long

Above: Three views of the castle published in Sir William Dugdale's Antiquities of Warwickshire (1656), engraved by Wenceslaus Hollar and based on Dugdale's own sketches. They capture the exterior of the castle in its heyday, with battlemented skylines. The top view focuses on John of Gaunt's buildings and the apartment ranges; in the middle and lower views, Leicester's Building is to the left and the keep to the right

Right: This depiction of the castle on a plate, made for the Empress Catherine of Russia in 1775 by Wedgwood, indicates the growing fame of the ruins at Kenilworth

Below: A Victorian lithograph, by John Brandard, depicting the 1575 entry of Elizabeth and Leicester into the castle, inspired by Sir Walter Scott's novel. A credible reconstruction of Leicester's Building and the east front of the inner court is in the background

Facing page: A late 19th-century photograph of two farm workers posed before the ruins of Lunn's Tower, typical of the souvenirs sold to Victorian visitors. The lower part of the inner court was a farmyard at this period

description of its history. Dugdale's work formed the basis of all subsequent histories of Kenilworth until the later 19th century, including the nomenclature used for many of its buildings, such as Lunn's Tower, Mortimer's Tower and Leicester's Building (see page 33). The slighting eventually took place in the summer of 1650, when the north side of the keep was demolished and various sections of the outer curtain destroyed.

Colonel Joseph Hawkesworth, the Parliamentarian commander who had overseen the slighting, acquired the estate in lieu of back payments for the local militia. He retained the castle for himself and converted Leicester's Gatehouse into a residence, which in due course became the house for a farm established in the lower part of the outer court. His fellow officers divided the estate into farms for themselves. The residential buildings of the inner bailey were pillaged for building materials, and the castle rapidly became a roofless ruin, with its fittings and fixtures reused in houses all round the area. At this time or shortly after, the mere was drained and the Inchford Brook returned to its natural course through a culvert in the dam.

In 1660 Hawkesworth was evicted at the Restoration of King Charles II (1660–85), when the castle was restored to Charles's mother, Henrietta Maria, and for a short time to the stewardship of the earls of Monmouth. In 1665 it was granted to Laurence Hyde (1642–1711), a brother-in-law of James, duke of York (the future King James II). In the 18th century the castle descended through his Hyde successors, then to Thomas Villiers, who became 1st earl of Clarendon of the second creation in 1776. It remained with the earls of Clarendon until 1937.

FROM ROMANTIC RUIN TO HISTORIC MONUMENT: 1800 TO THE PRESENT DAY

Tourists had begun to take an interest in the picturesque ruins of Kenilworth by the later 18th century. The first guidebook, *A Concise Guide and Description of Kenilworth Castle*, was published locally in 1777, and 25 editions of it had appeared by the 1840s. However, it was the publication in 1821 of Sir Walter Scott's romantic novel, *Kenilworth*, which established the castle as a major tourist attraction. Scott took liberties with history to tell a good story, having the life and suspicious death of Leicester's first wife, Amy Robsart (who actually died in 1560), played out against the background of Elizabeth I's visit in 1575. Nevertheless, Scott also conveyed a convincing evocation of the castle – the 'huge pile of magnificent castellated buildings, apparently of different ages' – which he knew from first-hand acquaintance. Many thousands of visitors were drawn to see the ruins, including Charles Dickens (1838), Queen Victoria (1858) and Henry James (1870s). Lord Clarendon kept 'an aged protector' on site to deal with visitors and sell souvenirs.

At the start of the 19th century, the ruins were allowed to decay, and in August 1817, 30 tons of stone crashed down from the north-west turret of the keep. When Scott revisited the castle in 1828, he found it 'better preserved and protected', perhaps as a consequence of the

Kenilworth in the 1930s

From Tea at the Castle: Kenilworth in the 1930s *by Philip Hames* (Odibourne Press)

'When I was a boy we lived in Leicestershire in a large house with a big collection of antiques. In the late 1920s my family read that the gatehouse of Kenilworth Castle was to let. They decided to rent it and open it up to the public; the antiques we had would give the impression of a small stately home. We took about 25 visitors around at a time and charged one shilling each.

'At times I had the job of taking the tour. The first room entered was the dining hall, with a large table, suits of armour, and the names of the guards engraved on the left-hand side: 'Henry Butler 1649' and 'Edward Ayworth 1620'. The staircase, removed from elsewhere in the castle, led into the oak room, which was entirely panelled in oak with a large oak four-poster bed.

'At the top of the stairs was my room. When I first moved in I woke with a bad headache every morning and then found that the floor was on such a slope I had to put eight-inch blocks at the head of the bed.

'Outside the gatehouse was the barn built by Lord Leicester for stables with its fine Spanish chestnut beams. We had the idea of making it into a restaurant. It was a great success. Conducted motor-coach tours were just starting then, and they nearly all visited us. Some of the big Midland car manufacturers used to send their new cars to be photographed in the grounds.

'In front of the barn were the remains of an old wall and together with the agent to the earl of Clarendon and the curator of the castle, we started to excavate this and found what we believed to be the remains of an old chapel, which was eventually identified as the 14th-century chapel of St Mary. As we could only do this in our spare time, we never finished it, but it caused a great deal of interest and was mentioned in the papers.'

'When I was a boy...my family read that the gatehouse of Kenilworth Castle was to let'

Below: Serving wenches in Elizabethan dress at 'Lord Leicester's Barn Restaurant' in the early 1930s

Right: Repairs in progress on the great hall in the second half of the 19th century. The ground level in the foreground is considerably higher than today

Below: A view of Leicester's Gatehouse from the south-west, by Moses Griffiths, about 1779. The room over the porch was removed in the early 19th century. Lunn's Tower (right) is still shown with its back wall, which collapsed about 1800 (compare the later photograph on page 51)

interest shown after the publication of his novel. Later in the century the growing appreciation of ruins as ancient monuments, combined with the destructive aspects of mass tourism, led to efforts to arrest the decay of the castle's buildings and to investigate their history more scientifically. Foremost among the proponents of such an approach was the local antiquarian, the Revd E H Knowles, whose book, *The Castle of Kenilworth* (1872), was the first modern, analytical account of the castle. His work benefited from clearances of rubble and restoration works undertaken in the 1860s. Whereas for many visitors 'the beauty of the ruins was heightened by the ivy which grows so luxuriantly' (Sarah Sargant, 1828), for Knowles the ivy was 'the crowbar of the giant' and 'must go'.

Substantial restorations continued in the late Victorian period and between 1926 and 1936 Lord Clarendon spent a further £10,000, but found he could not keep up with the maintenance required. So in 1937 the castle was purchased for the nation by the local motor industry magnate, Sir John Siddeley (1866–1953), who was created 1st Lord Kenilworth in the same year. He retained the gatehouse to live in, but placed the castle in the guardianship of the Commissioners of His Majesty's Works in 1938, giving a sum of £5,000 towards the cost of necessary repairs. In 1958 his son, the 2nd Lord Kenilworth, gave the castle to the town of Kenilworth, and the Town Council remains the legal owner. In 1984 English Heritage – the distant successor of His Majesty's Office of Works – became responsible for the care of the castle, and manages and maintains it today.